A Smart Kid's
Guide to
Personal Finance

How to Earn Money

Ryan Randolph

PowerKiDS press.

New York

Published in 2014 by The Rosen Publishing Group, Inc.
29 East 21st Street, New York, NY 10010

First Edition

Editor: Jennifer Way
Book Design: Greg Tucker

Library of Congress Cataloging-in-Publication Data

Randolph, Ryan P.
 How to earn money / by Ryan Randolph. — 1st ed.
   p. cm — (A smart kid's guide to personal finance)
 Includes index.
 ISBN 978-1-4777-0741-8 (library binding) — ISBN 978-1-4777-0823-1 (pbk.) —
 ISBN 978-1-4777-0824-8 (6-pack)
 1. Finance, Personal. I. Title.
 HG179.R3236 2014
 332.024—dc23
                            2012041865

Manufactured in the United States of America

CPSIA Compliance Information: Batch #S13PK5: For Further Information contact Rosen Publishing, New York, New York at 1-800-237-9932

Contents

Why Earn Money?

Do you have money in your pocket? How did that money get there? It may have been a gift. It could be money you earned by doing some **chore** or job. Some kids receive **allowances** from their parents. That allowance may be given so that kids can practice **budgeting** their money.

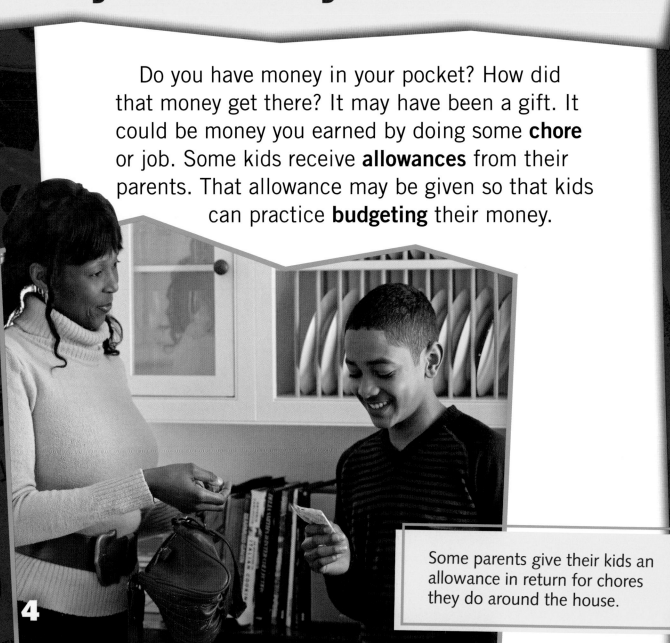

Some parents give their kids an allowance in return for chores they do around the house.

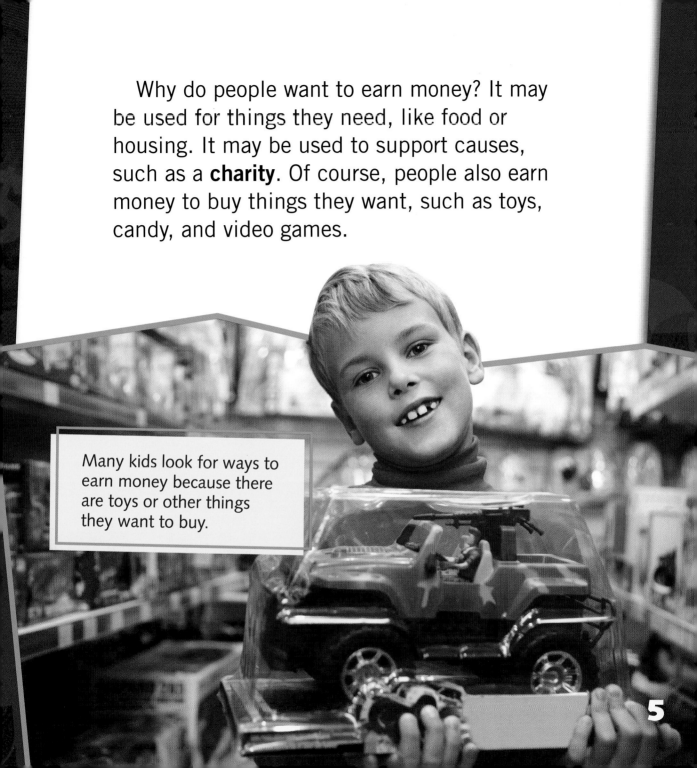

Why do people want to earn money? It may be used for things they need, like food or housing. It may be used to support causes, such as a **charity**. Of course, people also earn money to buy things they want, such as toys, candy, and video games.

Many kids look for ways to earn money because there are toys or other things they want to buy.

Earning Money Doing What Interests You

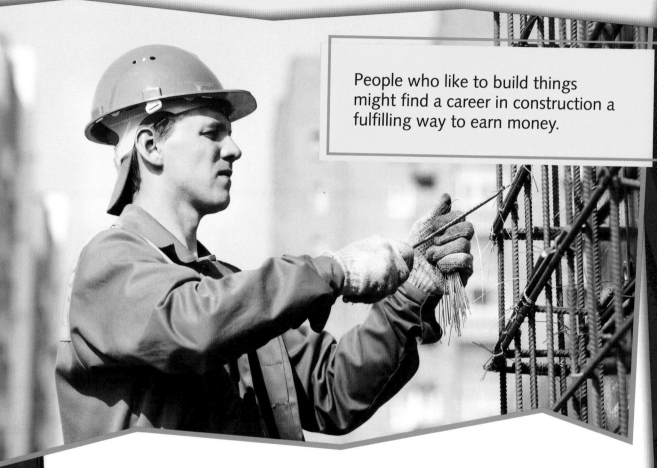

People who like to build things might find a career in construction a fulfilling way to earn money.

Adults earn money at their jobs. When you work at a job as an adult, hopefully it will be doing something you enjoy. Are you a hands-on person who likes to make things? Being a carpenter, chef, or mechanic may be a good **career** for you.

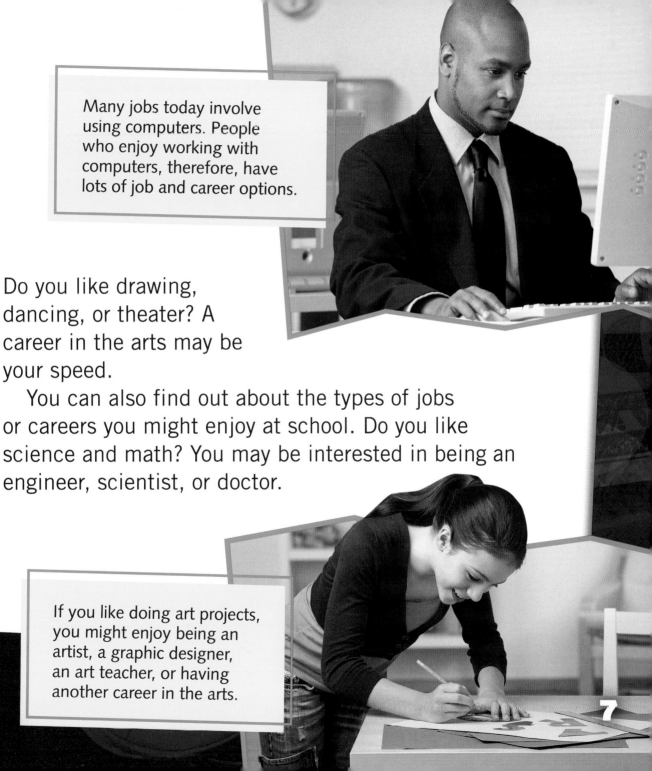

Many jobs today involve using computers. People who enjoy working with computers, therefore, have lots of job and career options.

Do you like drawing, dancing, or theater? A career in the arts may be your speed.

You can also find out about the types of jobs or careers you might enjoy at school. Do you like science and math? You may be interested in being an engineer, scientist, or doctor.

If you like doing art projects, you might enjoy being an artist, a graphic designer, an art teacher, or having another career in the arts.

7

Finding Ways to Earn Money

In most places in the United States, you cannot do many jobs until you are between 14 and 16, and some jobs you cannot do until you are at least 18. What can you do to earn money today?

Your parents or neighbors may have extra chores that need to be done that they would be willing to pay you to do. For example, if you clear the dishes from the table, ask your parents if you could wash them for extra money. You may have to learn how to do the extra work. Like adults, once you learn a new skill, it can help you earn money.

If you have elderly neighbors, they may have household chorcs or yard work that they would be willing to pay you to do.

Start Earning More Money Now!

Is there a subject in school that you are great at? You might be able to earn money by tutoring your classmates.

Do you enjoy making things? You could make money by selling things that you made. For example, if you enjoy baking cupcakes, you could try selling them. You might be able to do this in front of your house or at a local event.

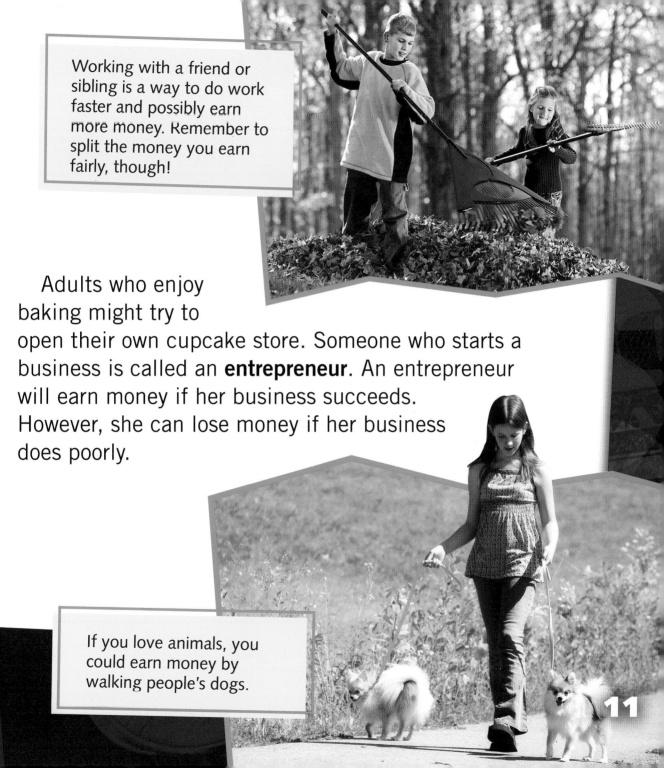

Working with a friend or sibling is a way to do work faster and possibly earn more money. Remember to split the money you earn fairly, though!

Adults who enjoy baking might try to open their own cupcake store. Someone who starts a business is called an **entrepreneur**. An entrepreneur will earn money if her business succeeds. However, she can lose money if her business does poorly.

If you love animals, you could earn money by walking people's dogs.

Ways of Getting Paid

If you make and sell crafts, you make money from each item sold. Make sure your prices cover the cost of materials you use as well as the time it takes to make your crafts!

People can get paid different ways. Most jobs pay hourly rates. This means more money can be earned by working more hours. Other jobs have **salaries**. Workers who get salaries are paid set amounts no matter how many hours they work.

Some workers are paid **commissions**. Commissioned workers are paid based on the amount they sell, not the hours they worked. Salespeople are sometimes paid on commission. Some people are paid **piecework**, or based on how much they produce.

The jobs that adults do sometimes earn them benefits as well as money. One benefit included in many jobs is health insurance.

Where Does the Money Go?

Local taxes pay for things that cities need, such as firefighters. Some local taxes are deducted from adults' paychecks.

Have you ever wondered who pays for the roads, parks, public schools, police officers, and firefighters we depend on? Our national, state, and local governments pay for these things. Where do these governments get the money to provide us with these things? They get it in part from the **taxes** we pay.

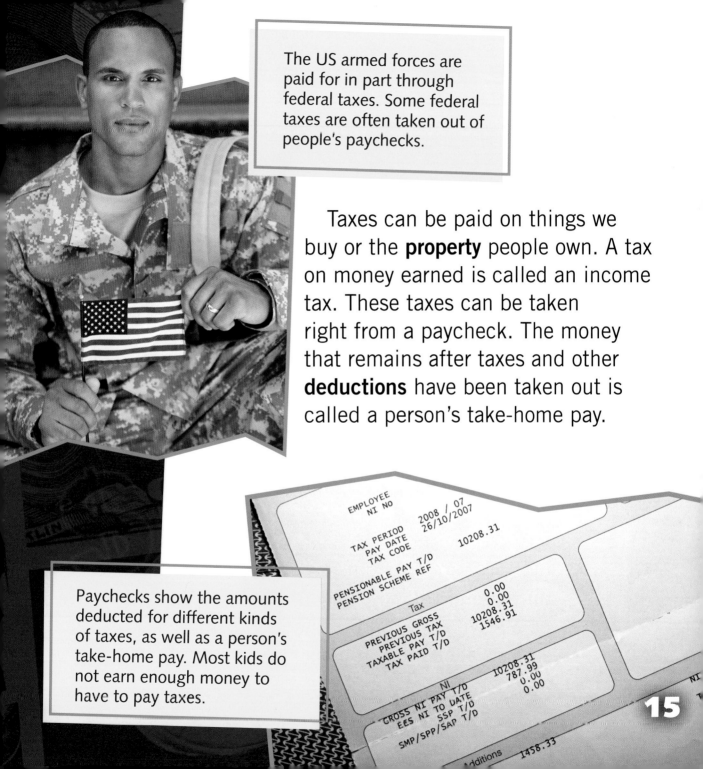

The US armed forces are paid for in part through federal taxes. Some federal taxes are often taken out of people's paychecks.

Taxes can be paid on things we buy or the **property** people own. A tax on money earned is called an income tax. These taxes can be taken right from a paycheck. The money that remains after taxes and other **deductions** have been taken out is called a person's take-home pay.

Paychecks show the amounts deducted for different kinds of taxes, as well as a person's take-home pay. Most kids do not earn enough money to have to pay taxes.

EMPLOYEE
NI NO

TAX PERIOD 2008 / 07
PAY DATE 26/10/2007
TAX CODE 10208.31

PENSIONABLE PAY T/D 0.00
PENSION SCHEME REF 0.00

Tax 10208.31
PREVIOUS GROSS 1546.91
PREVIOUS TAX
TAXABLE PAY T/D
TAX PAID T/D

NI 10208.31
787.99
CROSS NI PAY T/D 0.00
EES NI TO DATE 0.00
SSP T/D
SMP/SPP/SAP T/D

Additions 1458.33

15

Spending and Saving Smartly

Making a budget helps you use the money you earn wisely. It can help you reach financial goals, too. For example, let's say that saving money for a bike is your goal. Instead of spending all of your money right away, a budget helps you decide to spend only a little of your earnings. Then you can save the rest of your money to buy a bike.

Some people find it helpful to put their spending money and savings in different places. You could put the money in different envelopes, or your parents may be able to help you put the money in a savings account at a bank.

If you are saving up for a bike, making a budget can help you figure out how long it will take you to meet your goal.

Take It to the Bank

Putting money in a bank is another way to save and earn money. Sometimes banks will pay you a little bit to keep your money in a savings account. This is called **interest**, and interest earns money for you.

Your parents can help you open a savings account. Banks charge fees for some services.

Using an ATM is a way that many adults manage their money on the go.

It is smart to see what the fees are at a few different banks before opening an account at one. Most adults use banks for both saving and spending. Besides going to the bank, they use checks, ATMs, and **debit cards** to keep track of their money.

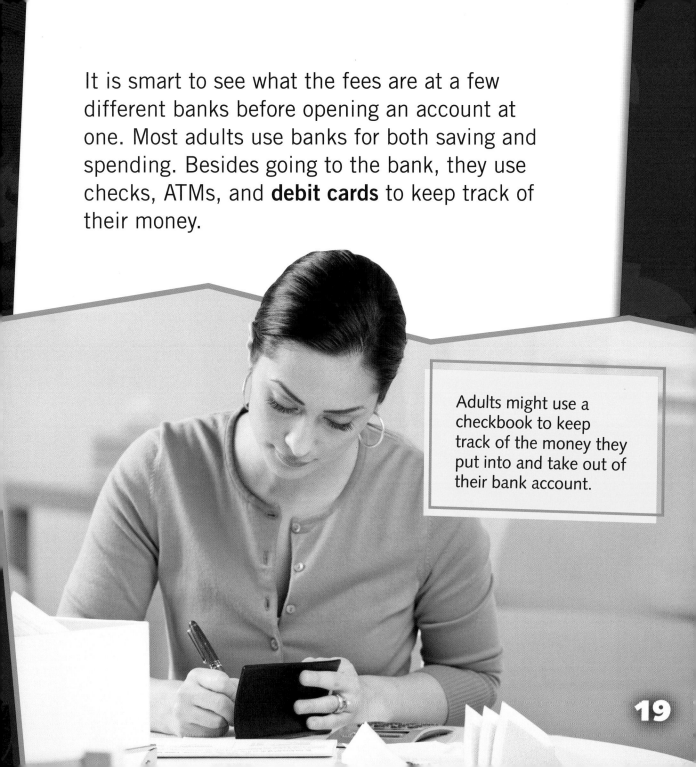

Adults might use a checkbook to keep track of the money they put into and take out of their bank account.

Be Smart About Money

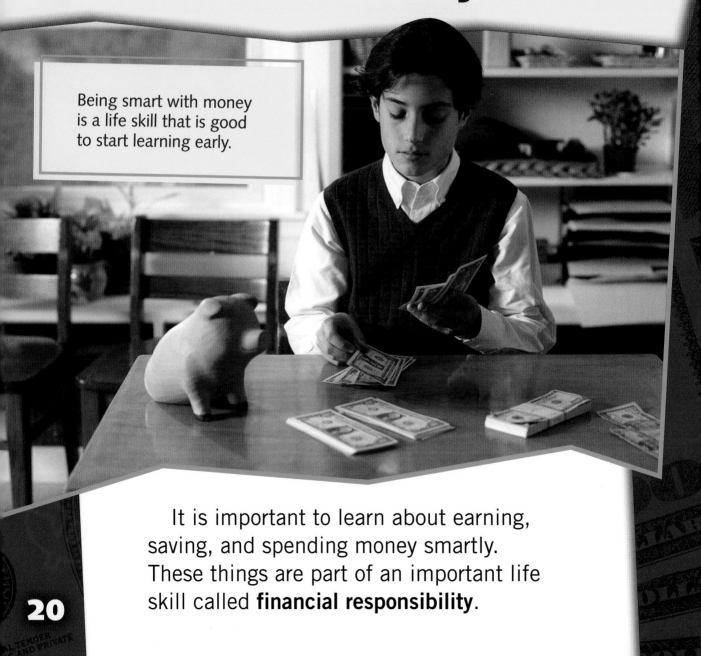

Being smart with money is a life skill that is good to start learning early.

It is important to learn about earning, saving, and spending money smartly. These things are part of an important life skill called **financial responsibility**.

Sometimes the things we want or need cost more than we have saved. To get these things, you need to try to save more money, earn more money, or do both. Once you earn money, you need to decide how to spend it or to save it. Making a budget and developing good spending and saving habits will help you manage your money. Learning about the skills and tools that will help you become financially responsible are the first steps to using money smartly!

Many people use their computers to create and manage their budgets. A parent or another adult can show you how to get started doing this.

Money-Earning Tips

1. If your family has a yard sale, ask if you can sell toys, books, or other things you no longer use. You can put the money you make toward something you are saving for.

2. You might be able to earn money by building on the chores you already do at home. If you already put the laundry away, offer to wash, dry, and fold it, too.

3. Help your parents or neighbors plant flowers in the spring and weed in the summer. You can rake leaves in the fall and shovel snow in the winter.

4. There may be a place near you that offers cash for recyclable cans and bottles. Each can or bottle is worth only a few cents. If you collect a lot, the money adds up, though!

5. When your neighbors go on vacation, you could make money by offering to do things such as collect their mail, feed and walk their pets, or water their plants or garden.

Glossary

allowances (uh-LOW-ents-ez) Money given regularly to people.

budgeting (BUH-jit-ing) Planning to spend a certain amount of money in a period of time.

career (kuh-REER) A job.

charity (CHER-uh-tee) A group that gives help to the needy.

chore (CHOR) A task that people perform daily.

commissions (kuh-MIH-shunz) Fees paid to people for doing services.

debit cards (DEH-but KAHRDZ) Cards used to pay for things or to take money out of accounts.

deductions (dih-DUK-shunz) Amounts taken out of other things.

entrepreneur (on-truh-pruh-NUR) A businessperson who has started his or her own business.

financial responsibility (fuh-NANT-shul rih-spont-suh-BIH-luh-tee) Using money wisely and well.

interest (IN-teh-rest) The extra money that the bank pays someone with a savings account.

piecework (PEES-wurk) Work done and paid by the piece.

property (PRAH-pur-tee) Land or buildings owned by people.

salaries (SAL-reez) Fixed amounts of money paid to workers.

taxes (TAKS-ez) Money added to the price of something or paid to a government for community services.

Index

Websites

Due to the changing nature of Internet links, PowerKids Press has developed an online list of websites related to the subject of this book. This site is updated regularly. Please use this link to access the list: www.powerkidslinks.com/skgpf/earn/